21st Century Skills **INNOVATION LIBRARY**

# MINDSTORMS: Level 2

Peachtree

**CHERRY LAKE PUBLISHING • ANN ARBOR, MICHIGAN**

by Rena Hixon

CHERRY LAKE Publishing

A Note to Adults: Please review the instructions for the activities in this book before allowing children to do them. Be sure to help them with any activities you do not think they can safely complete on their own.

A Note to Kids: Be sure to ask an adult for help with these activities when you need it. Always put your safety first!

Published in the United States of America by Cherry Lake Publishing
Ann Arbor, Michigan
www.cherrylakepublishing.com

Reading Adviser: Marla Conn, Read With Me Now
Photo Credits: Cover and page 1, ©PRNewsFoto/The LEGO Group; pages 4, 6, 11, 12, 13, 15 ,16 ,19, 21, 24, 26, 27, and 28, Rena Hixon; page 8, ©Tiramisu Studio/Shutterstock

Library of Congress Cataloging-in-Publication Data
Hixon, Rena, author.
  Mindstorms. Level 2 / by Rena Hixon.
     pages cm.—(21st century skills innovation library. Unofficial guides)
  Audience: Grades 4 to 6.
  Includes bibliographical references and index.
  ISBN 978-1-63470-525-7 (lib. bdg.)—ISBN 978-1-63470-645-2 (pbk.)—
ISBN 978-1-63470-585-1 (pdf)—ISBN 978-1-63470-705-3 (ebook)
1. LEGO Mindstorms toys—Juvenile literature. 2. Robotics—Juvenile literature.
3. Detectors—Juvenile literature. 4. Computer programming—Juvenile literature.
I. Title.
  TJ211.2.H485 2016
  629.8'92—dc23                                2015030340

Cherry Lake Publishing would like to acknowledge the work of The Partnership for 21st Century Skills. Please visit www.p21.org for more information.

Printed in the United States of America
Corporate Graphics
January 2016

**21st** Century Skills INNOVATION LIBRARY

# Contents

Chapter 1

# The Sonar Sensor

f you're reading this book, you probably already know about some of the incredible things you can do with Lego Mindstorms. You may even have built some Mindstorms robots yourself. Hopefully you know what the different parts do, how to make a basic program, and how to use the EV3 programmable brick. If not, you should start by reading *Unofficial Guides: Mindstorms Level 1*. Then come back to this book once you're ready!

Adding sensors to your projects will greatly expand what you can do with Mindstorms.

The focus of this book will be learning how to use **sensors** in your Mindstorms projects. Sensors collect information about their environment. They send this information to the EV3 programmable brick. The EV3 responds to the information in different ways depending on how it is programmed. For example, you might create a program that allows a robot to detect and avoid obstacles.

There are two different Mindstorms EV3 kits available for purchase. The retail kit comes with a color sensor and a touch sensor. The education kit has those sensors, too. However, it also includes an **ultrasonic** sensor and a **gyro** sensor. The retail kit has an **infrared** sensor and a remote control that can be used with it.

This book covers the color sensor, touch sensor, ultrasonic sensor, and infrared sensor. The gyro sensor is more complex than the others. If you want to learn more about it, check out the other books in this series.

Let's start by learning how to use the ultrasonic sensor. This is the one that looks like it has round red eyes. It is commonly referred to as the **sonar** sensor.

This is because it works a lot like the sonar ability used by bats. A bat can send out special sound waves. You can't hear them, but they bounce off nearby objects and return to the bat. The bat then knows how far away different objects are, how fast they are moving, and which direction they are heading in. The Mindstorms sonar sensor uses a similar technique to determine the distance of objects.

The sonar sensor has two round, red "eyes."

You can learn a little about the sonar sensor before you use it to build a robot. Attach a sonar sensor to one of the four **input ports** on the EV3. The input ports are labeled 1, 2, 3, and 4. It doesn't matter which one you use right now.

On the EV3, select the **icon** with six small circles, then choose the "Port View" option. Now choose the port number of the attached sonar sensor. You should see the readings of the sensor measured in centimeters. Pick up the sonar sensor and move it around. See what types of readings you get. You should notice that the number goes up the farther the sensor is from an object. Moving the sensor closer should make the number go down. Try to get the number as high and low as possible. In theory, the lowest number that you should be able to read is 0. However, you will find that it is very difficult to get a reading of 0. The smallest you can detect will likely be around 4 centimeters. The largest reading you can get is 255 centimeters.

The EV3 can also display sensor readings in inches. To try this out, hit the middle button on the EV3 while still viewing the port. It will display three options: "US-DIST-CM", "US-DIST-IN", and "US-Listen". Select "US-DIST-IN". Check the minimum and maximum values that you can read in inches. Again, you should

## Sensors All Around

Sensors like the ones used in Mindstorms projects are all around you. These devices are common parts of many everyday devices. Have you ever used a touchless sink or hand dryer in a public bathroom? These devices use sensors to detect when your hands are near.

Another place you might find sensors is on your family car. It is common for newer vehicles to include sensors that detect cars or other objects around them. They then alert the driver so he or she can react to avoid an accident.

be able to get a reading of 0 in theory, but you will find it difficult to get anything lower than about 1.2 inches. The maximum reading is 100.3 inches.

It is time to build a robot and see what you can do with the sonar sensor! You can find directions for building a simple robot at *www.damienkee.com/ home/2013/8/2/rileyrover-ev3-classroom-robot-design.html*. Follow these instructions and attach the sonar sensor.

Now you are going to program a robot to avoid objects. Open the Lego Mindstorms EV3 software and start a new program. When your sonar sensor detects an object, you want your robot to turn away from it. Then you want it to keep doing this over and over again, until you get tired of watching it and turn it off!

In order to make a robot do something over and over again, you need to create something called a loop. You will find the "Loop" icon under the light-orange button. Bring that into your program. The **default** is for an unlimited loop. This means the loop will never end until you turn off the robot.

The next icon you need is "Move Tank". Add it to your program and place it inside the loop. Set it to turn on motors B and C. Do not specify a distance on your motors. You want them to stay on until the sonar sensor detects an object. So the next icon you are going to use is "Wait". This icon is also under the light-orange button. Once you've added it to your loop, you have to tell it what to wait for. Choose "Ultrasonic Sensor" and select "Compare Inches". Don't forget to select the port your sonar sensor is plugged into.

You can program the EV3 to check for measurements that are *equal to*, *not equal to*, *less than*, *less than or equal to*, *greater than*, or *greater than or equal to*. You can choose *less than* or *less than or equal to* for this experiment. The distance is under the rectangle icon with a red dot. The smaller the number you choose, the closer your robot will get to an object before turning. As you discovered earlier, you should not use a number smaller than 4 centimeters or 1.2 inches.

The next thing you need to do is program your robot to turn when it gets too close to an object. It does not matter which direction it turns. Bring a "Move Tank" icon into your loop. Choose whichever settings you want. Think back to the activities in the previous book in this series. Do you remember how to make your robot turn at different speeds?

Below is an example of what a finished program should look like. The sonar sensor is attached to port 2, and the motors are attached to **output** ports B and C. Download the program to your EV3 and run it. Your robot should move forward and turn to avoid any objects in front of it. Try sending your robot through a maze. Then see if you can keep it from falling off a table.

**Chapter 2**

# The Infrared Sensor

N ow that you know how to use the sonar sensor, let's try out the infrared sensor. Start by attaching the infrared sensor to a port. Select the "Port View" option just as you did with the sonar sensor. What do you notice about the values it displays? While the sonar sensor read in centimeters and inches, the infrared sensor measures distance

The infrared sensor looks somewhat like the sonar sensor, but with narrower "eyes."

from 0 to 100. A value of 0 means an object is very close. A value of 100 means the object is far away.

Go back to the program you created in chapter 1. You can replace the "Wait" for ultrasonic with a "Wait" for infrared. Your robot should perform a lot like it did with the sonar sensor. However, the sensor works differently to accomplish its job. Remember that the sonar sensor uses sound waves that you can't hear. Instead, the infrared sensor uses light waves that you can't see. While the infrared sensor can be used to measure distance like the sonar sensor, it can also do other things.

Port View provides important information about your sensors.

For example, the infrared sensor can be used along with a remote control. The Mindstorms remote has four different channels, numbered 1 through 4. Channel 1 is when the red switch is pushed up as far as it can go toward the black end of the remote. Channel 2 is the next position down, then 3, and then 4. The program determines which channel is used with your robot. If you use channel 3, another robot can use one of the other channels. This would allow you to switch between two robots using the same remote. If you put two robots with infrared sensors on the same channel, you can control them both at the same time. The program for each robot could tell it to do something different than the other one.

A program can be used to assign functions to each of the remote's buttons. Suppose you want to use the remote to control the motors on your robot. You could use one button to make the right motor go forward and another to make the motor go backward. You can also program more complicated controls. For example, you might program the motors to turn off when two buttons are pressed at once. Open up the EV3 software and see if you can figure out how to program some basic remote controls for the robot you built in chapter 1. Below is one possible solution. Remember to make sure the channel is set correctly in your program. It needs to match the channel you are using on your remote.

## Incredible Infrared

You have probably used an infrared sensor before without knowing it. Most computer mice rely on infrared sensors to detect movement. The sensors send out infrared light from the bottom of the mouse. As a user moves the mouse across a surface, the sensors transmit information about its speed and position to the computer. This information moves the cursor around on the computer screen.

You can assign different functions to each of the buttons on the remote.

## Chapter 3

# The Color Sensor

N ext, let's try out the color sensor. This device has two main settings. It can be used to detect light, or it can be used to detect a certain color. When it is being used for color, this book will refer to it as a color sensor. When it is being used for light, it will be referred to as a light sensor. When using it as a light sensor, you will notice a red light on the device. If you use it as a color sensor, the light will be different.

Look at the light sensor before plugging it in. You will see two things that look like lightbulbs. One is quite a bit larger than the other one. Connect the sensor to the EV3 and select the "Port View" option. The default is for the sensor to measure reflected light. You should notice that the larger lightbulb is sending out a red light. This light reflects off of objects. The smaller bulb on the sensor reads this reflected light. The sensor can then determine how dark or light the object is.

Experiment with the light sensor. Try to figure out the maximum and minimum values that can be detected. Are dark colors lower values or higher values? What is the lowest value you can detect? What is the highest? You should find that dark colors reflect less light and give smaller values. You should have been able to detect 0 fairly easily. Light colors give larger values. If you found just the right object, you could read a value as high as 100. For example, you should hit 100 if you point the sensor at the EV3 unit from the right distance.

Press the middle button on the EV3 while in Port View. You will see three options: "COL-REFLECT", "COL-AMBIENT", and "COL-COLOR". Select "COL-COLOR". The sensor is now ready to detect color. Take a look at the sensor's larger bulb. You should notice that instead of sending out a red light, it now sends out different colors. Point the sensor at different colors of Lego pieces. You should notice that different colors cause the EV3 screen to display different numbers. A reading of 0 indicates that there is no color detected. Try to find out what colors relate to what numbers. How many did you find?

The color sensor's larger bulb emits light. The smaller one reads the light that is reflected back to the sensor.

The sensor can detect seven different colors:

0 = No Color

1 = Black

2 = Blue

3 = Green

4 = Yellow

5 = Red

6 = White

7 = Brown

Another light source you can experiment with is **ambient** light. Press the center button while in Port View, then select "COL-AMBIENT". In this mode, the light sensor is reading light in the room around it instead of light reflected from an object. The range of detectable values is 0 through 100 again. Move into darker and brighter rooms. You should see higher values in brighter areas and lower ones in darker areas.

Let's take a closer look at the reflected light readings. Set the sensor back to "COL-REFLECT". Lay the sensor flat on the surface of a black piece of paper and look at the reading on the EV3. Now try the same thing on a white piece of paper. It is probably going to be very close to the same value for both readings. Now try it again, but very slowly move your light sensor up from the surface of the paper. Pay attention to the readings as you go. You should notice that you get better differences between the white and black readings when the light sensor is about 0.25 to 0.5 inches (0.64 to 1.27 cm) away from the source. As the sensor gets farther away, it will detect less difference in the readings. Keeping this in mind, secure the sensor to the same robot you used in the previous chapters.

Now you are going to use the light sensor to keep your robot inside an oval shape. You will need a large

piece of poster board and some black electrical tape.
Use the electrical tape to make an oval on the poster
board. Set your robot on the poster board. Check the
values in Port View again. If they are not very different
between the white poster board and black tape, you
need to adjust the height of the sensor from the ground.

The program for this activity is going to be very
similar to the programs you wrote to make your robot
avoid objects. What do you think the main difference
will be? Instead of programming the robot to wait for
ultrasonic or infrared readings, you will program it to

Black tape on a white background is easiest for
your sensor to read.

## Let There Be Light

Have you ever been riding in a car in the evening and noticed the streetlights suddenly turn on? Unlike the lights in your home, streetlights aren't controlled by a simple switch. Instead, they use sensors to turn on and off automatically as needed. Once a light sensor detects when the natural light isn't bright enough to see, the streetlights turn on. When the light sensor notices that it is bright outside again the next morning, they turn off.

wait for dark readings. This is a little trickier than the previous programs. You have to find the exact dark value of the tape you used to make your oval. Use your sensor in Port View to do this. It is best to set your robot down just as it would be when running, in order to read the values. This will give you more accurate readings. Back in the EV3 software, set the value on the "Wait" icon to about five more than the value of the dark you detected.

Download the program to your robot and run it. How is it working? You might notice that the robot sometimes turns too quickly when it hits the black line. This could cause it to move outside of the oval. Adjust the values in your program if you need to.

By now you should have a feel for the values your program needs to detect the electrical tape. Let's try writing a program that makes your robot travel around the oval by following the tape with the light sensor.

Rather than following the tape itself, the robot will follow the line where the black tape meets the white poster board. Before creating your program, you need to choose which direction your robot is going to travel and which side of the line to follow. The side of the line you choose to follow will change the direction your robot turns. If the example program doesn't work, try placing the robot on the other side of the line.

To follow a line, you will need the light sensor to tell the EV3 whether it is detecting the black of the electrical tape or the white of the poster board. Then you need the EV3 to make sure the robot stays pointed along the edge of the black tape. If your robot detects black, it should turn toward the white. If it detects white, it should turn toward the black. This will cause your robot to jiggle back and forth as it travels.

Start your program with an unlimited loop. Place a "Switch" icon inside your loop. Select the light sensor and compare for less than a reflected light value. (You can use the same values from the previous oval activity.) Program the robot to turn left if true (check mark). Program it to turn right if false (x). An example of a working program is below. However, the light values and ports may be different from the ones you used.

Download and run your program to see if it works. You should be able to test if your robot is working by holding it over the black line and checking to see if the stopped motor switches when it sees the line. If this is not happening, make sure the icons in your program are correct. You can also check to make sure your motors are connected correctly.

Once the program is working, try making a variety of paths for your robot to follow. Use the same colors of poster board and electrical tape to create different shapes. Your robot should be able to follow any of these paths!

## Chapter 4

# The Touch Sensor

T he touch sensor is one of the simplest sensors in the EV3 kit. However, it has several important uses. Plug it in and access the Port View on the EV3. Play around with the sensor and keep an eye on the display. You might notice that there are only two possible values. If the sensor is pressed in, you will see a 1. If not, you will see a 0. That's it!

Let's write a program that makes your robot drive up to an object, touch the object, and stop. Start by mounting the sensor on the front of the robot. Can you write a program that will make your robot drive forward until the touch sensor is pressed? The first thing the program should do is turn on your motors. Now use a "Wait" icon and tell the robot to wait for a touch and turn off the motors.

Now let's try a program that makes your robot drive forward each time the touch sensor is bumped. What do you think the difference is between bumping and pressing the sensor? A bump waits for the touch sensor to be pressed and released before it performs an action. That means if you hold down the touch sensor, the EV3 will not do anything until you release it.

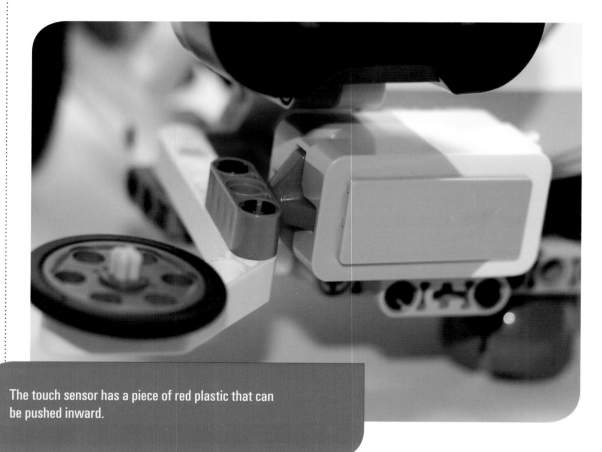

The touch sensor has a piece of red plastic that can be pushed inward.

Start your program with a "Wait" icon that waits for the touch sensor. Select "Compare State".

Now add the "Move Tank" icon. Turn on motors B and C for degrees. Set the "Degrees" measurement to 90. Finally, put a loop around all of the **code**. Download and run your program. When you press and release the touch sensor, the robot should move forward slightly.

The last experiment is going to be to drive forward until the touch sensor is bumped and then change directions. Start with a loop. Then add a "Move Tank" icon. Just as in the previous program, tell the robot to wait until the touch sensor is bumped. Then use a "Move Tank" with negative numbers on the

## What's Next?

Now that you know how to use the main sensors, you have a lot more options for creating your Mindstorms projects. What will you make next? Try building a remote-controlled car. Now try adding a sonar sensor and programming the car to stop moving anytime it gets close to a wall. You've created a remote-controlled car that can't crash! What other ways can you think of to combine the different sensors? Be creative, and don't worry if your ideas don't always work right away. Trying new things is the best way to improve your understanding of the Mindstorms system.

motors. This will make the robot go in reverse. Finally, tell the robot to wait until the touch sensor is bumped again. Download and run your program. Does it work like you planned? If you have any issues, check to make sure everything is connected correctly.

In this book, we have looked at the EV3's most commonly used sensors. Hopefully you are now comfortable avoiding objects with the sonar sensor, using the infrared sensor with a remote control, following a line with the light sensor, and detecting objects with the touch sensor. You should be able to use the programming language to control the robot using the information received from these sensors. Are you ready for the next steps?

# Glossary

**ambient** (AM-bee-uhnt) relating to the immediate surroundings of an object

**code** (KODE) instructions for a computer written in a programming language

**default** (di-FAWLT) a setting or option that will be effective if you don't specifically choose one in a computer program

**gyro** (JYE-roh) a sensor that can determine direction, tilt, speed, and movement; short for *gyroscope*

**icon** (EYE-kahn) a graphic symbol on a computer screen that represents a program, function, or file

**infrared** (IN-fruh-red) a color of light that cannot be seen by the human eye

**input** (IN-put) information fed into a computer

**output** (OUT-put) information produced by a computer

**ports** (PORTS) places on a computer that are designed for a particular kind of plug

**sensors** (SEN-surz) devices that measure light, sound, movement, and touch

**sonar** (SOH-nar) an instrument that sends out sound waves to determine the location of objects

**ultrasonic** (uhl-truh-SAH-nik) sounds that are too high for a human ear to detect

# Find Out More

## BOOKS

Bagnall, Brian. *Maximum LEGO EV3: Building Robots with Java Brains*. Variant Press, 2014.

Garber, Gary. *Instant Lego Mindstorms EV3*. Birmingham, UK: Packt Publishing, 2013.

Griffin, Terry. *The Art of LEGO MINDSTORMS EV3 Programming*. San Francisco: No Starch Press, 2010.

## WEB SITE

### Lego Mindstorms: Build a Robot
*www.lego.com/en-us/mindstorms/build-a-robot*
Check out instructions for building other Mindstorms robots.

# Index

## About the Author

Rena Hixon received a bachelor's degree in computer science from the University of Missouri–Rolla (now Missouri University of Science and Technology). She also earned a doctorate in electrical engineering from Wichita State University. She worked as a software design engineer for 11 years and has taught computer science classes at Wichita State for more than 13 years. In 2004, Rena and her husband started a Lego robotics club for homeschooled students. Its aim is to teach engineering principles, emphasizing math and science, to children. Rena has also taught her own Lego robotics camps for 12 years as well as camps at Missouri S&T for several years.